Fresh
Made
Simple

Fresh Made Simple

A NATURALLY DELICIOUS WAY TO EAT

Look » Cook » Savor

Lauren K. Stein *Illustrated by* Katie Eberts

Storey Publishing

The mission of Storey Publishing is to serve our customers by
publishing practical information that encourages
personal independence in harmony with the environment.

Edited by Margaret Sutherland
Art direction and cover design by Jeff Stiefel
Indexed by Nancy D. Wood
Illustrations by © Katie Eberts

The information in this book is true and complete to the best of our
knowledge. All recommendations are made without guarantee on the part of
the author or Storey Publishing. The author and publisher disclaim any liability
in connection with the use of this information.

Storey books are available for special premium and promotional uses and
for customized editions. For further information, please call 1-800-793-9396.

Storey Publishing
210 MASS MoCA Way
North Adams, MA 01247
www.storey.com

Printed in China by Toppan Leefung Printing Ltd.
10 9 8 7 6 5 4 3 2 1

Library of Congress Cataloging-in-Publication Data

Stein, Lauren K., author.
  Fresh made simple : a naturally delicious way to eat: look, cook, savor / By
Lauren K. Stein.
     pages cm
  ISBN 978-1-61212-608-1 (hardcover : alk. paper)
  ISBN 978-1-61212-609-8 (ebook) 1. Cooking. 2. Snack foods. I. Title.
TX652.S697 2015
641.5—dc23
                    2015020327

For Abigail —
you inspired this book,
little bear.

— *Lauren K. Stein*

For Dolores,
Roxanne & Joanne —
love you all to the moon & back

— *Katie Eberts*

Contents

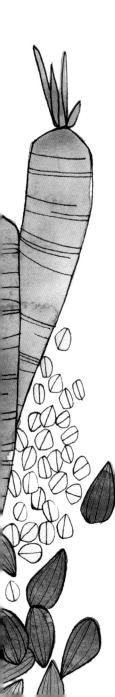

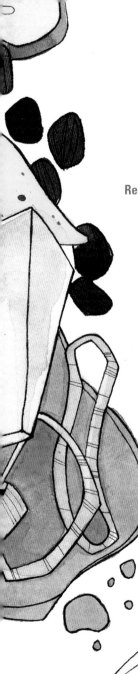

162   Cheesy

Red Leicester Cheese	Red Leicester Cheese Plate
Blue Cheese	Blue Cheese Plate
Robiola	Robiola Cheese Plate
Pecorino	Cacio e Pepe
Halloumi	Grilled Halloumi
Fontina	Fondue
Ricotta	Honey Ricotta Crostini
Mozzarella	Ricotta Mozzarella Melt

180   Plain Vanilla

Cantaloupe	Cantaloupe, Blueberries & Vanilla Bean Ice Cream
Apple	Apple Pie Ice Cream
Pineapple	Grilled Pineapple with Ice Cream & Caramel
Raspberry	Raspberry Spinach Parfait

Introduction

Fresh Made Simple is a beautiful reminder that we don't need much to enjoy food. A handful of ingredients and a pretty picture will do. Some good company is nice, too.

I dreamed up this book when my constant dining companion was this tiny, opinionated, cute but messy eater named Abigail. My daughter hit the 6-month mark and we were off and eating: sweet potatoes, bananas, avocado, mango, and apples were among her first bites. Feeding her fresh, whole foods was a reminder that more of the food I was eating should look like the food she was eating.

Aside from sleeping, much of our time together was devoted to eating and reading. Being together in the kitchen and amongst her books inspired me to craft a food idea book for both of us to enjoy. When it looks good, I want to eat it. When it tastes good, I want more. When it is fresh and healthy, I feel good. Didn't others, including my little girl, feel the same way? If the ingredients were fresh, colorful, and accessible, and the preparation simple and illustrated, cooks of all ages and skills could enjoy the recipes. So, an illustrated guide to enjoying simple, fresh food — truly everyday eating — was born. These are not complicated recipes — there is very little text, and the beautiful illustrations guide the cook. The point is: it is pretty hard to mess up these foods, so I hope you have fun experimenting in the kitchen, just like I did. Add more lemon for zing, cut down the garlic if it's not your favorite, substitute nut milks if you don't drink dairy. Most important, taste as you go and enjoy the flavors and colors.

To get this book done, I made a mess in the kitchen, and then illustrator Katie Eberts put my words and cooking to paper with her stunning watercolor and ink drawings. Katie was able to capture in her pictures the fun and whimsy and freshness of cooking. And she made them instructional, too. In my opinion, food has never looked so good!

Katie and I met when we were both contributing to Eat Boutique, whose founder, Maggie Battista, played matchmaker when I told her about my idea for an illustrated food book. Katie and I have been long-distance cooking and drawing together for the last year and a half to get this book ready. It's safe to say the recipes taste and look equally as good in Boston (my home base) as they do in Michigan (Katie's neck of the woods) and in a lot of different spots in between (where all our testers live)!

Features of This Book

There are so many ways to enjoy this cookbook, no matter your age or cooking skills. Put it out on your coffee table and flip through it for food inspiration. Let your guests flip through it and enjoy the illustrations. Encourage your kids to read it and pick out something to make together. Keep it propped up on a recipe stand in the kitchen for when you need an idea for a quick and simple bite to eat. Drop it in your bag on the way to the farmers' market to see what is fresh today.

I've organized the book by the form or texture of the recipe — Smashed, Stacked, Tossed, Cheesy, etcetera — just because it was more fun than the usual breakfast, lunch, and dinner. Some recipes can be eaten at any meal, while others are perfect snacks. I snuck in a few sweet items, too. The left pages highlight a particular ingredient — a fresh fruit, vegetable, herb, nut, or cheese, for example — that is used in a simple recipe on the facing page. Each page offers tips, ideas, and some general instructions for preparing and enjoying the food. But really the idea is to let the illustration guide you.

Simple recipes mean that the dishes can be prepared pretty quickly. The food ideas illustrated on these pages are forgiving and are mostly based on loose measurements — a handful of this, a dollop of that — giving you freedom to tailor the ideas to suit your tastes. Add more or less of each component (for me, it's always more garlic!), or toss in a spice or condiment or ingredient you know and love. Make bigger batches for a crowd or pare it down to dine solo. Add chicken or beef or shrimp or tofu to many of these recipes to make a heartier meal.

Most of the recipes require just a handful of ingredients. Most of the time, the foods you need will be on hand or easy to find in a grocery store. Depending on the season, your nearby farmers' market will be a wonderful resource. I was inspired for so many of

the recipes by the beautiful fresh vegetables that came in my farm share over the summer. Fresh (and, if you can, local) food tastes so good on its own; you don't need to add much to it. I pair flavors and colors and foods that taste good together and keep it easy.

And eating with my daughter continues to inspire me — I want her to love food of all kinds, and I don't want to make separate dishes for each member of the family; I don't have time to. Sometimes I eat the entire dish and she eats some of the components. No, she hasn't tried all the recipes. But yes, I hope she does one day.

This is not a kids' cookbook, but it is a cookbook to use with your kids. The recipes are easy, the ingredients are fresh, and the illustrations mean that even youngsters can follow the recipes without reading the text. When my toddler helps me pick

11

out the food and participates in the cooking, she tends to be a much more willing eater. She plucks grapes off the stems and washes them under the faucet. We make trail mixes together: she opens all the different containers of nuts and dried fruit, asks me "What's this one, Mama?" and then tosses some in a little baggie. She is constantly dragging her stool around the kitchen to be near the food preparation. Working on this book made me realize that it was a good idea to let cooking together spill right over to dinner together at the table whenever possible. It is definitely not a sure thing that she will eat what we have made, but at least we are having fun together trying.

I have spent years filling up my kitchen with immersion blenders and cast iron skillets, with vegetables from a farm share, with wine glasses and cookbooks, and more recently with sippy cups and high chairs. I love to go out to dinner. I watch cooking shows on television and read food magazines. I don't intend to give any of it up (except maybe the sippy cups and high chairs, at some point). I think food and eating and being in the kitchen is fun. Add to that mix work and meetings and play and phone calls and all the things we keep busy with each day. Thankfully, there's room in the fridge for just a few more ingredients and space on the shelf and time in my day for *Fresh Made Simple*, too.

Some Reminders

All the recipe ideas include fresh food. Please wash the produce and if needed peel or trim the fruits and vegetables before getting started. I have not put specific instructions for these steps in each recipe. Some foods shouldn't be consumed by very young children; please follow instructions from your health care practitioner when introducing food. And while I encourage cooking with kids, please be vigilant around the oven, stove, blenders, and knives. Little helping hands love to grab . . . anything!

Stocking My Fresh Kitchen

Creating this book gave me the opportunity to truly recognize the foods I love to have on hand in the kitchen. Here's my short list.

LEMONS or LIMES: for dressings, guacamole, salsa, tacos, water, and because they look pretty in a big bowl

AVOCADO: at least two because sometimes I pick bad ones; for salads, for guacamole, on toast, or plain

NUTS: for surprise guests, snacks, trail mix, granola, dessert toppings, and salads

GREENS: a bag of spinach or kale means you always have a handful of something green to toss in smoothies and with eggs

HUNK OF CHEESE: for snacks, alongside soups, in a melty sandwich

ONIONS: because I just love to sauté them and throw them in so many things

EGGS: for breakfast, lunch, or dinner; with or without cheese and veggies, hard-boiled, scrambled, and over easy are my favorite preparations

PLAIN GREEK YOGURT: my daughter gobbles it down for a quick snack, and it's my usual substitute for mayo or sour cream

BREAD: the good crusty kind from your local bakery, just because

BUTTER: the good kind, to go with the bread

BANANAS: to eat with peanut butter, in smoothies, in sandwiches, with ice cream and oatmeal, and as an on-the-go snack

SALT: Morton's coarse kosher salt for most things, in a tiny little dish on the counter, with a sea salt grinder, too, for when it needs to be super fine

For more of my tips and recipe ideas like the ones in this book, visit www.laurenkstein.com.

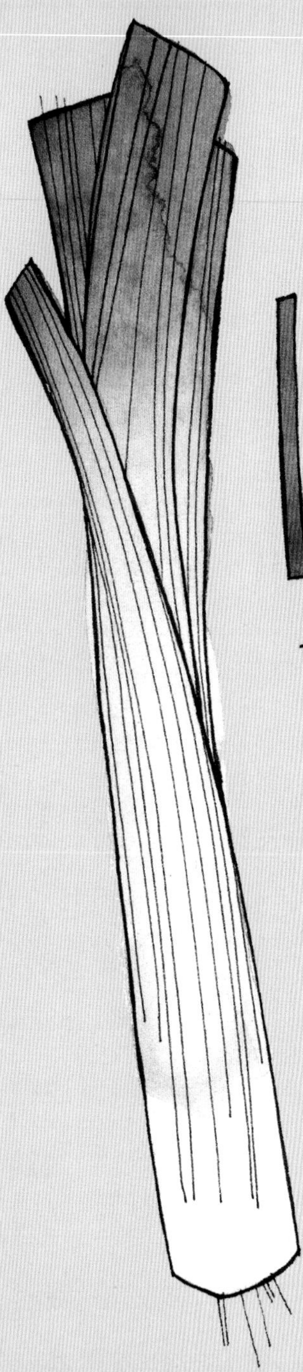

LEEK

the dark green tops
look cute sticking out
of your market bag,
but stick to the white
& light green parts
for this egg bake.

Whole milk

One big leek or two small ones

Fresh or Frozen

Salt & Pepper

LEEK CORN EGG BAKE

Goat cheese

Bake at 325°F for 40 minutes or until eggs are set.

Grease first

Mushroom

A funny little fungus that tastes so good with so many things: risotto, pizza, eggs, quesadillas, ravioli...

Salt & Pepper

Cheddar cheese

Raw or Sautéed (page 77)

SPINACH

Sauté until wilted & drain in a clean cloth.

1
2
3
4
5

¼ cup Milk

MUSHROOM SPINACH EGG BAKE

POUR into a greased pie plate & bake at 325° F for 35–40 minutes, until eggs are set.

Scallion

Scallions are a pretty garnish that add a mild onion flavor to many dishes.

tortilla

Drain first & add a handful.

BLACK BEANS

Salt & Pepper

Cook for a minute, then add eggs.

Scramble & cook through.

CHEDDAR

Melted butter

Burrito Scramble

Top with scallions, diced tomato, a dollop of plain Greek yogurt & some Cheddar.

Green Bean

Forget breakfast,
green beans & egg
make the
best dinner.

Kale

Kale kind of goes with everything: Smoothies, Salads, Pasta, Pesto...

Egg

A little egg, a little cheese,
a little green — any combo will do.

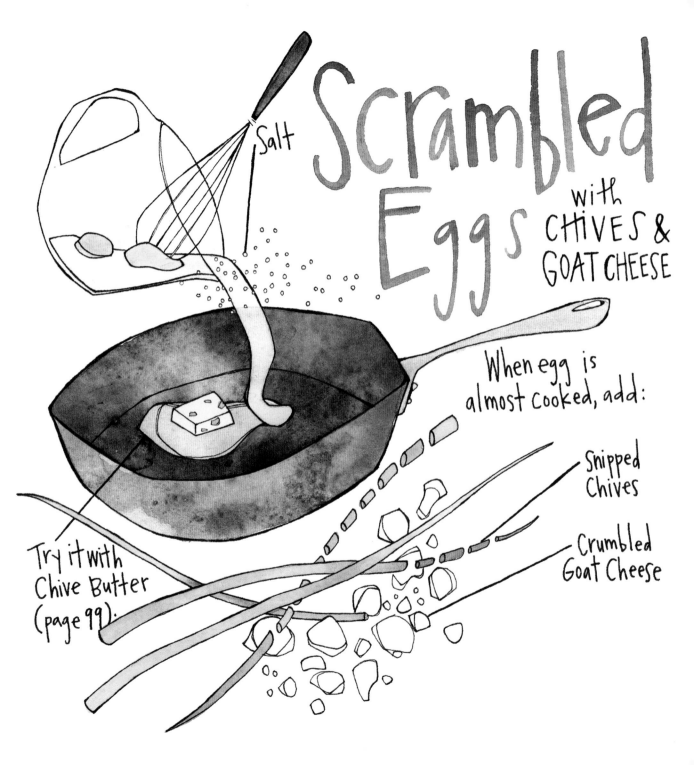

Salt

Scrambled Eggs
with CHIVES & GOAT CHEESE

When egg is almost cooked, add:

Snipped Chives

Crumbled Goat Cheese

Try it with Chive Butter (page 99).

KALE

There is no shame in hiding your veggies in a smoothie.

Any milk you like

1 cup Milk

KALE
STRAWBERRY
BANANA
SMOOTHIE

BLEND

Banana

Bananas and peanut butter are a classic combination for this smoothie. Toss in some spinach or kale for a surprise twist (and an extra helping of veggies!).

Spoonful of cocoa powder

Banana

Almond or Peanut butter

Whole milk

Blend with an immersion blender.

1 CUP

Chocolate Banana Nut Smoothie

Kale

When you get lots of extra greens from the farm or garden, make pesto and freeze it for later. Spinach, arugula, and cilantro also make delicious pesto.

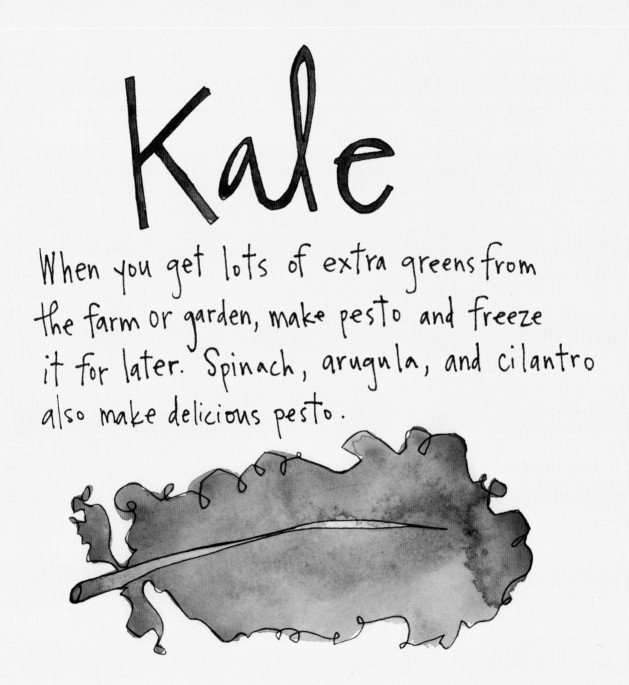

Lots of fresh Parmesan

olive oil

A bunch of toasted pine nuts

Big squeeze

Sprinkling of salt

garlic

Blend, adding olive oil as needed for desired consistency.

Try a giant handful of baby kale.

Kale PESTO

Drinking in the aroma of fresh ginger
is half the fun of making this dressing.

Hoisin Sauce

Water

1-inch piece of fresh ginger, peeled & grated

a couple swirls

sprinkle of Sesame oil

SOY GINGER DRESSING

Lime

Keep limes out on the counter in a big bowl: they look pretty and they are so useful.

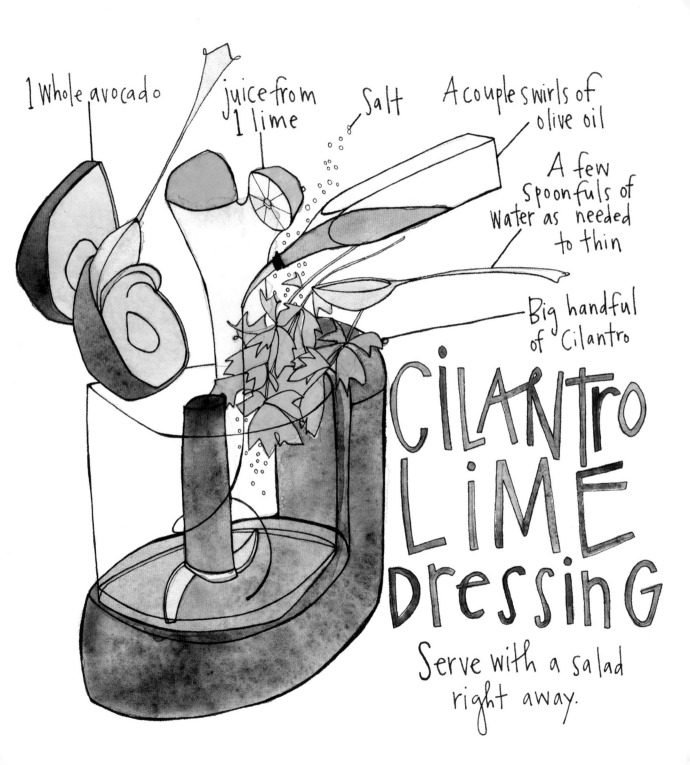

1 Whole avocado

juice from 1 lime

Salt

A couple swirls of olive oil

A few spoonfuls of water as needed to thin

Big handful of Cilantro

CILANTRO LIME DRESSING

Serve with a salad right away.

HONEY

Squeeze it from a plastic bear or drizzle it with a pretty dipper. Either way tastes sweet.

APPLE

Homemade applesauce is easy. Use Gala apples year-round or whatever variety you pick fresh from the orchard in the fall.

5 big apples
& 1 pear, peeled
& diced

Cook, uncovered,
on MED/HIGH
heat until
mushy, about
15 minutes, then
mash up right in
the pan.

APPLE-
SAUCE

stir
occasionally.

Cover the
bottom with
water, about
½ inch.

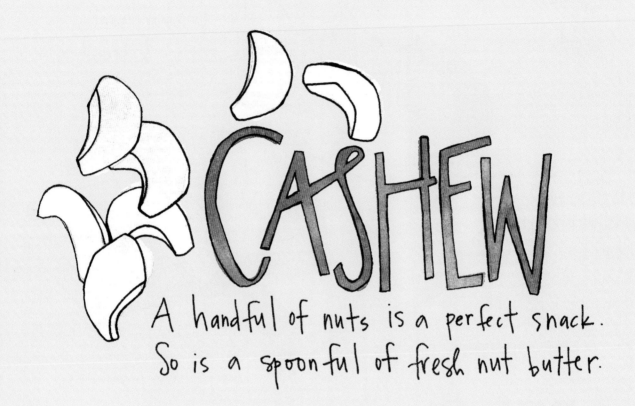

CASHEW

A handful of nuts is a perfect snack.
So is a spoonful of fresh nut butter.

AVOCADO

Green is
GOOD:
Avocado
Cilantro
Jalapeño

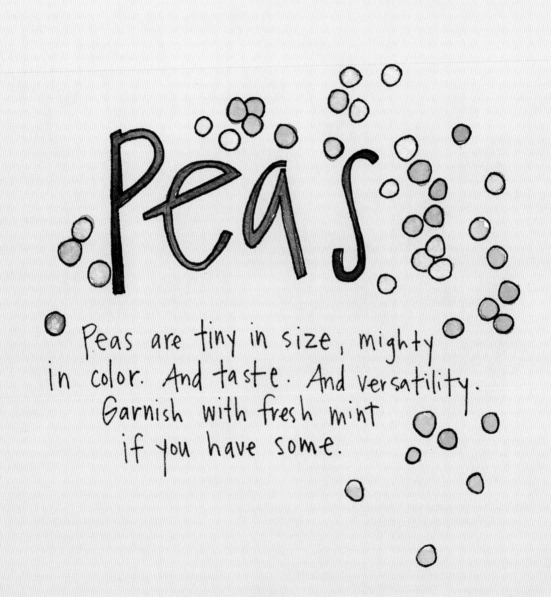

Peas

Peas are tiny in size, mighty in color. And taste. And versatility. Garnish with fresh mint if you have some.

Steam the peas.

Blend half of the peas with salt & a little water until smooth.

Pea Purée & Linguine

Pea Purée

freshly steamed peas

toasted pine nuts

Fresh linguine, cooked according to package directions

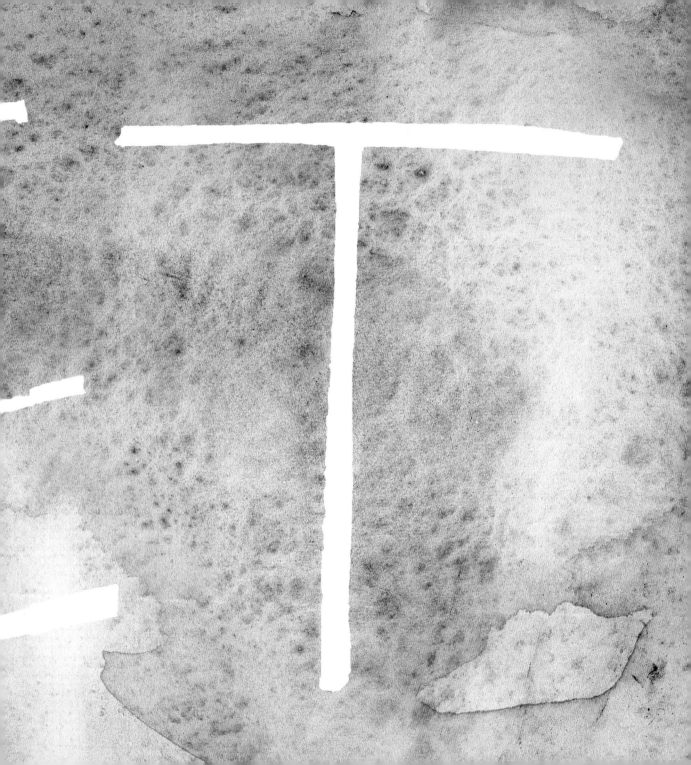

PEACH

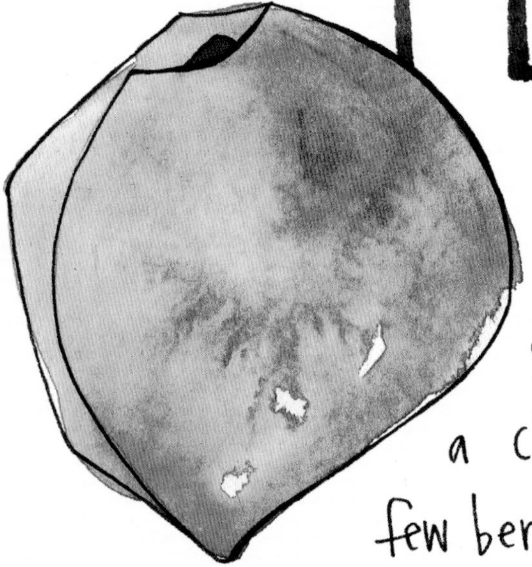

The fruit & mint look
G O R G E O U S
swimming together in
a clear pitcher. Or drop a
few berries, peach slices, and
mint leaves into individual glasses.

mint leaves

handful of blueberries, mashed

One peach, peeled & sliced

PEACH
mint & blueberry
WATER

Water & ice

CHILL BEFORE SERVING.

WATERMELON

Combinations for flavored water are endless.
Why not watermelon & strawberries?

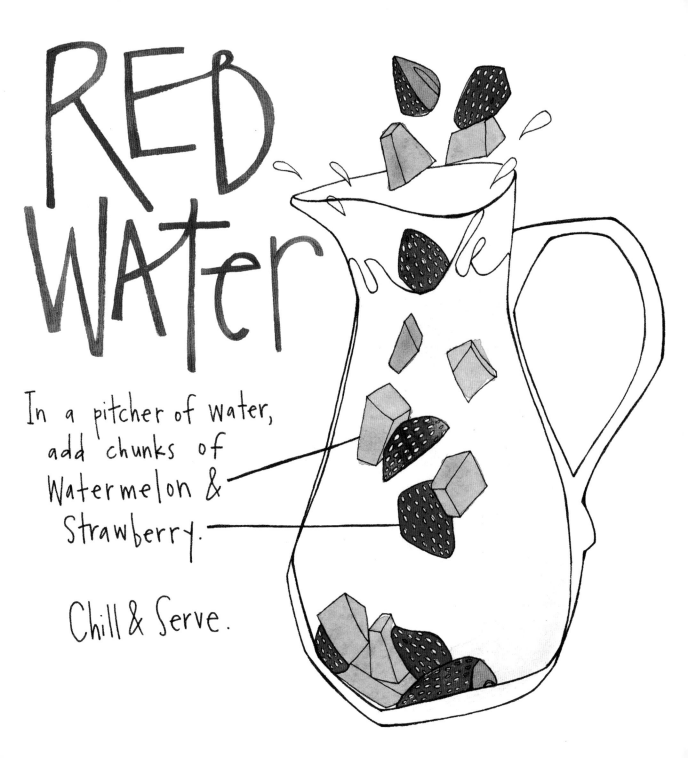

RED WATER

In a pitcher of water, add chunks of Watermelon & Strawberry.

Chill & Serve.

Mint

Give yourself a spa day at home, starting with a refreshing glass of flavored water.

Minty Cucumber Water

Mint leaves

Half a cucumber, peeled & sliced

Garnish with a squeeze of lime juice in each glass.

Chill.

ORANGE

Citrus brightens everything. Make this colorful pitcher your next centerpiece.

Citrus Water

Half an orange & two small lemons, sliced

Chill before serving.

WATERMELON

A summer side dish is as easy as
watermelon on a pretty platter.
This salad is just a few steps more.
Either is delicious.

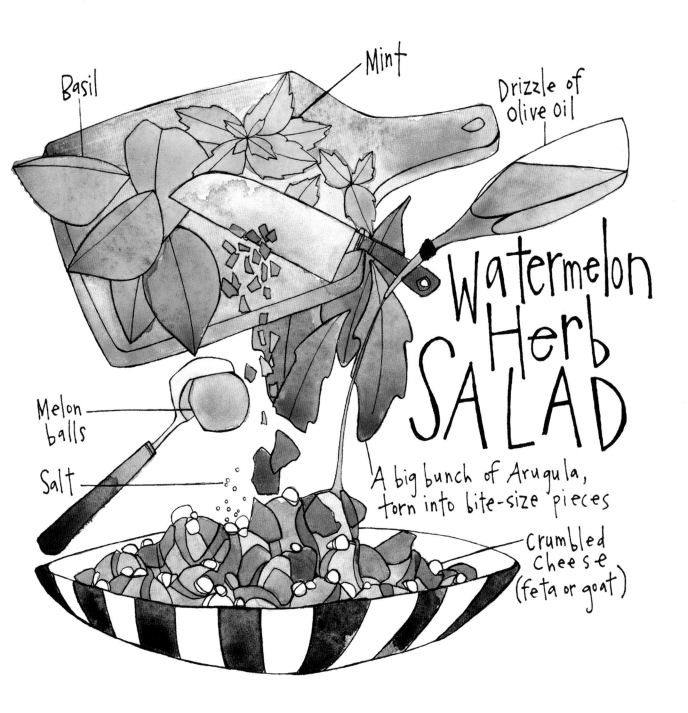

Basil

Mint

Drizzle of olive oil

Watermelon Herb SALAD

Melon balls

Salt

A big bunch of Arugula, torn into bite-size pieces

crumbled cheese (feta or goat)

Apple

Apple plus Manchego tastes really good in the backyard on a summer night with a glass of something cold.

Apple Manchego SALAD

Cut an apple & a chunk of Manchego cheese into matchsticks
(leave the skin on the apple for color).

Squeeze some lemon juice on top.

Tender onions
+
Crispy greens
+
Salty cheese
=
One perfect side salad

Spinach

A healthy swirl of olive oil for sautéing

Red onion, Sautéed until tender

Crumbled Feta cheese

Baby Spinach

Warm onions will soften the cheese and wilt the spinach just a tiny bit.

SPINACH Salad

Pistachio

Already shelled pistachios are great to keep on hand for nut mixes, ice cream toppings, and just a quick handful here and there.

Raisins

Honey Roasted Sesame Sticks

Dried Cherries

Roasted, unsalted & shelled Pistachios

Give a shake to mix.

Pistachio Nut Mix

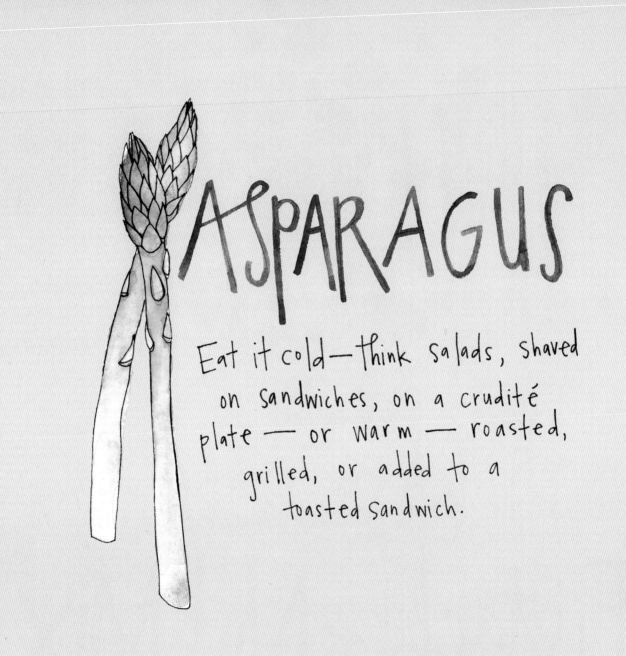

ASPARAGUS

Eat it cold—think salads, shaved on sandwiches, on a crudité plate — or warm — roasted, grilled, or added to a toasted sandwich.

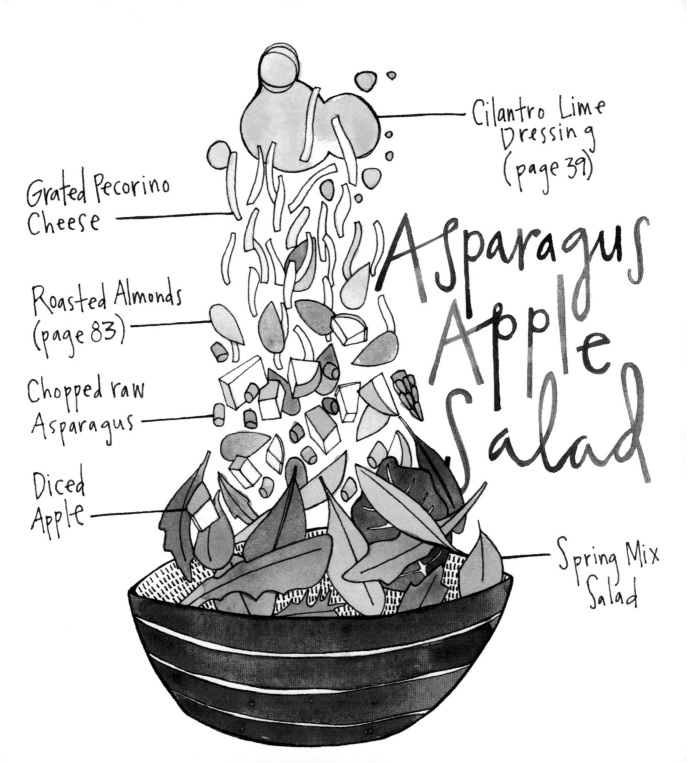

Cilantro Lime
Dressing
(page 39)

Grated Pecorino
Cheese

Roasted Almonds
(page 83)

Chopped raw
Asparagus

Diced
Apple

Asparagus
Apple
Salad

Spring Mix
Salad

Lettuce

See what's fresh at the market. The base for this salad is up to you.

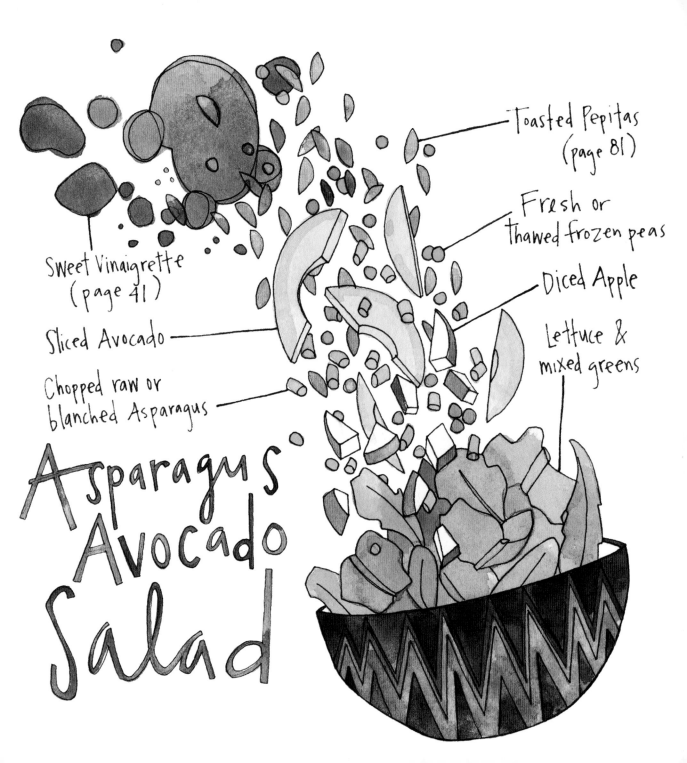

Toasted Pepitas
(page 81)

Fresh or
thawed frozen peas

Diced Apple

Lettuce &
mixed greens

Sweet Vinaigrette
(page 41)

Sliced Avocado

Chopped raw or
blanched Asparagus

Asparagus
Avocado
Salad

MUSHROOM

Mushrooms add umami — that hard-to-
describe-but-can't-get-enough-of-it savory taste —
to even the simplest dishes.

Sautéed Mushrooms

Sliced mushrooms

finely diced Shallot

Butter

Sauté for 5 minutes over medium heat, until tender & browning.

Pour into a bowl (or over pasta or greens) and top with a dollop of fresh ricotta & chopped fresh parsley.

Pepitas

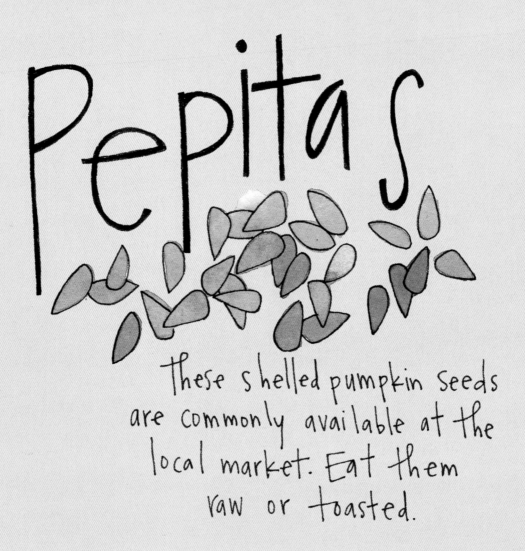

These shelled pumpkin seeds
are commonly available at the
local market. Eat them
raw or toasted.

Toasted Pepitas

Roast in a 400° F oven for 6–8 minutes until just browning. Immediately toss with a small pat of butter & finely ground salt. Let cool & enjoy!

Roasted nuts smell like
winter & the holidays.
Plus, it's a nice way
to warm up the kitchen.

ALMOND

Roasted ALMONDS

Spread raw, blanched almonds on a cookie sheet & roast in a 400°F oven for 6-8 minutes until just browning. (KEEP AN EYE ON THEM!)

Toss immediately with a small pat of butter & salt.

Serve with honey for dipping.

POTATO

You might find that the golden skin
of this potato is your favorite bite.

OATS

Homemade granola = Sticky

Salty

Sweet

Crunchy

Nutty

Fun

1 teaspoon
Vanilla

1 tablespoon
coconut oil

4 tablespoons

PURE MAPLE SYRUP

1/3 cup

unsweetened
coconut flakes

raw macadamia
nuts, roughly
chopped

pinch of
salt

1 cup
rolled oats

SPREAD out

on a cookie sheet
& bake at 300°F
for about 25 minutes,
OR
until golden.

Mix together
with your hands.

Granola

RED Pepper

Cooking with color just feels good. And red peppers are a great source of vitamin C. Try different-colored veggies for different nutrients.

Rub with olive oil.

Broil skin-side up until charred.

Remove the seeds & slice into quarters.

ROASTED RED PEPPER

Let cool & peel skin off.

GARLIC

Always keep garlic on hand. Raw or sautéed, its fragrant punch is so important in so many dishes.

Baguette

Pick up a baguette — or another crusty bread such as sourdough, French, Italian, or ciabatta — at the bakery and then get some really good butter or olive oil.

that's all.

CROSTINI

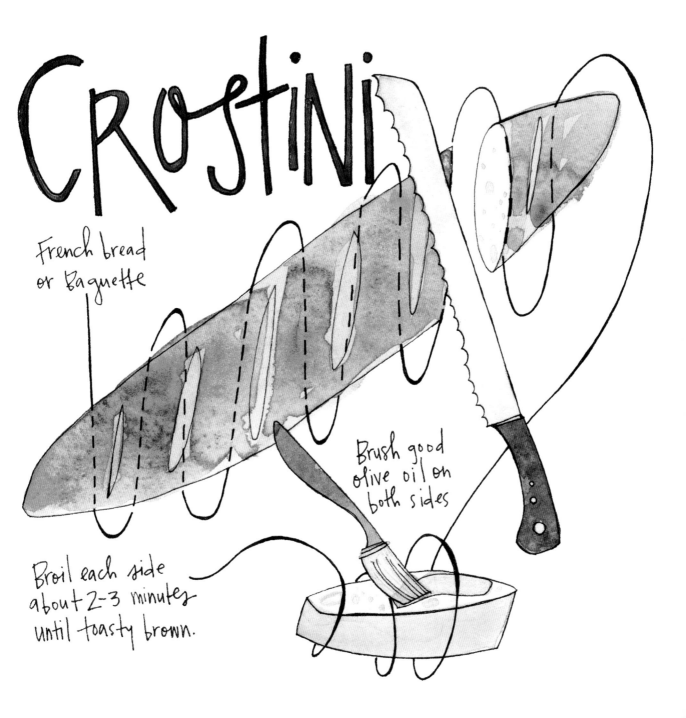

French bread
or baguette

Brush good
olive oil on
both sides

Broil each side
about 2-3 minutes
until toasty brown.

GINGER

There aren't many things better than flavored butter slathered on a toasty muffin. The spicy kick from ginger pairs just right with the sweet honey for this butter, but ginger can be used with savory foods, too.

GINGER LEMON HONEY BUTTER

just a squeeze

zest

Salt

Room temperature butter

Blend well & refrigerate for 1 hour.

Toast both halves of a corn muffin until there are nice brown marks. Slather on the butter & let it get melty.

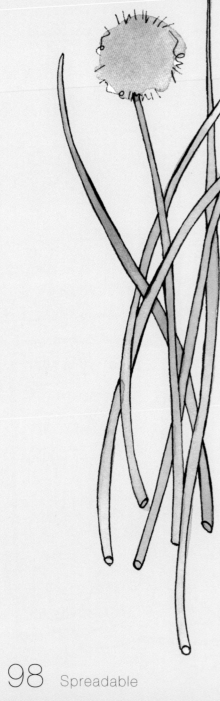

CHiVE

Try growing chives in a window box just outside your kitchen. You'll find many uses for their light onion flavor.

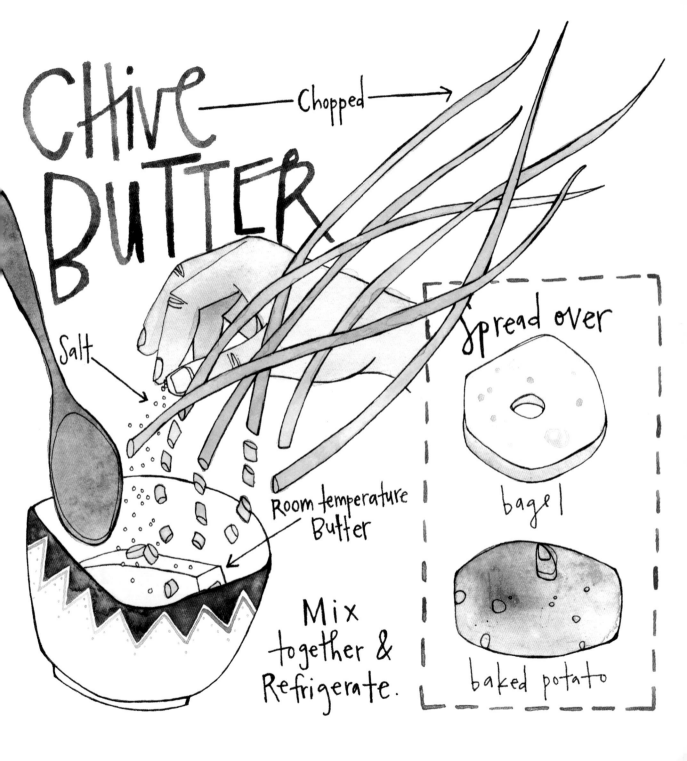

ZUCCHINI

Summer's zucchini crop can seem
ENDLESS.
Seek out zucchini recipes all year so
you'll be ready when the bounty arrives.

Grated Zucchini (Drain in a clean dishcloth.)

Chopped Carrots

Veggie cream Cheese

Mix together.

Room temperature cream cheese

Serve with crackers, bagels & cucumber slices.

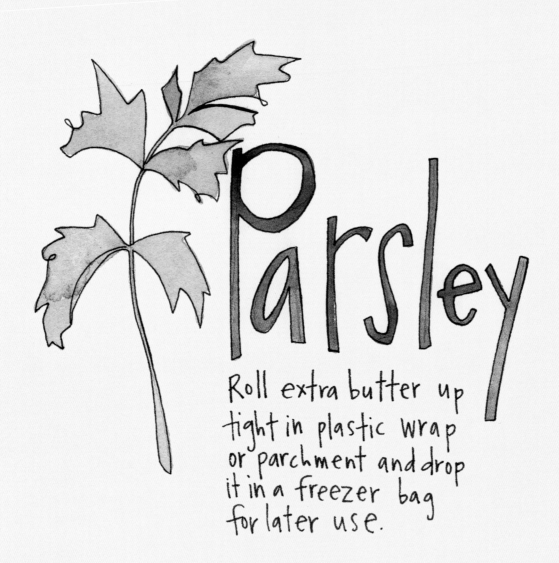

Parsley

Roll extra butter up
tight in plastic wrap
or parchment and drop
it in a freezer bag
for later use.

finely chop

Parsley
(a big bunch)

Basil

Scallions

Garlic

Room temperature butter

Mix thoroughly

and put in the fridge
for one hour.

Herb Butter

Try this on noodles, toast,
a potato, or a steak.

CHEDDAR

Cheddar might be basic,
but basic can taste so good.

Sharp Cheddar Cheese, 4 oz., shredded

1 Roasted Red Pepper (page 89)

Salt

Enjoy immediately as a dip, or refrigerate for spreading later.

CHeDDaR PePPer Spread

OFF | LOW | HiGH | PULSE

Pulse until spreadable.

Avocado

Scoop. Smash. Spread.
Avocado toast plus a fried egg
works any time of day.

Salt

Lime

EGG AVOCADO TOAST

Fried

Multigrain Bakery Bread

TOMATO

Let this juicy summer staple **SHINE**, no mozzarella needed.

TOMATO SLICES

Slice a ripe farm tomato.
Drizzle olive oil.
Sprinkle Salt & Pepper.

Cucumber

Wouldn't you like to find a
Cucumber & Tomato Sandwich
in your lunch box?

Cucumber & Tomato Sandwich

Olive oil

Salt & Pepper

Toast

cream cheese

Sliced cucumbers & tomatoes

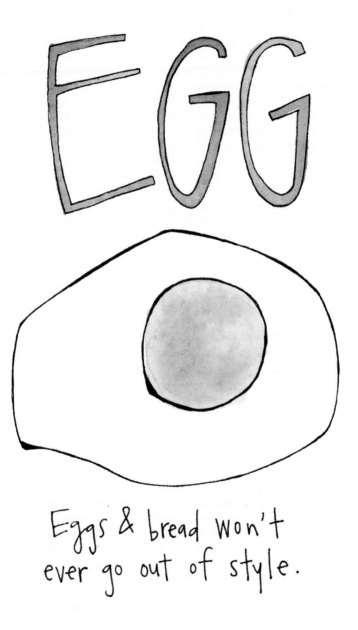

EGG

Eggs & bread won't ever go out of style.

Roasted Red Pepper

Roasted red peppers
are the perfect
secret weapon veggie.
Sneak them into dips,
Sauces, and warm sandwiches.

Red Pepper
Goat Cheese
MELT

Butter

Try Sourdough

Arugula

Roasted Red
Pepper
(page 89)

Goat Cheese

Let both sides get brown
and the cheese melty.

Feta

Add some shredded chicken
or beef to your tostada
and it's a complete meal.
Avocado & tomato on hand?
Toss them on, too!

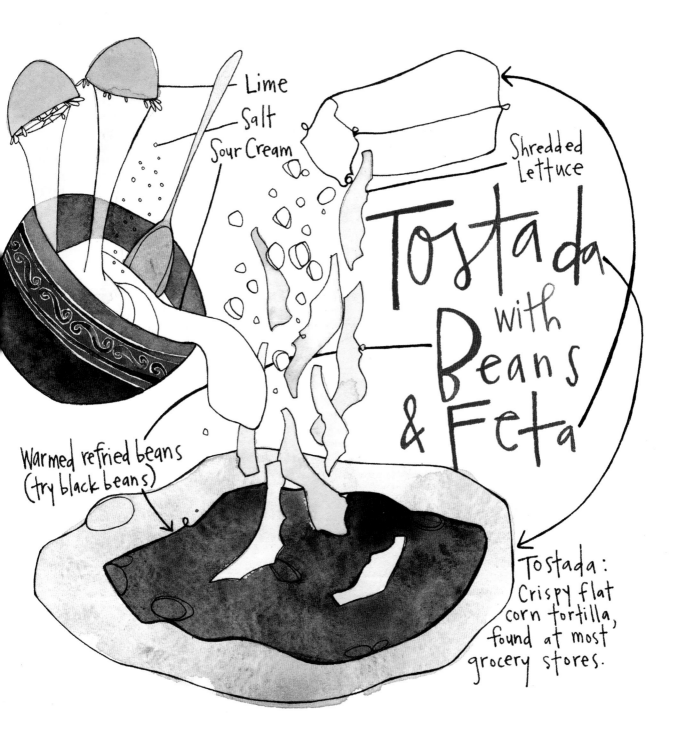

Lime
Salt
Sour Cream

Shredded Lettuce

Tostada with Beans & Feta

Warmed refried beans (try black beans)

Tostada: Crispy flat corn tortilla, found at most grocery stores.

EGG

Keep a few hard-boiled eggs on hand for really quick lunches.

Salt & Pepper to taste

Hard-boiled egg

Avocado

Mixed Greens

Thousand Island Dressing

Toasted Sourdough

OPEN-FACED EGG & AVOCADO

PEAR

That first juicy bite of just-ripe pear is so worth the wait.

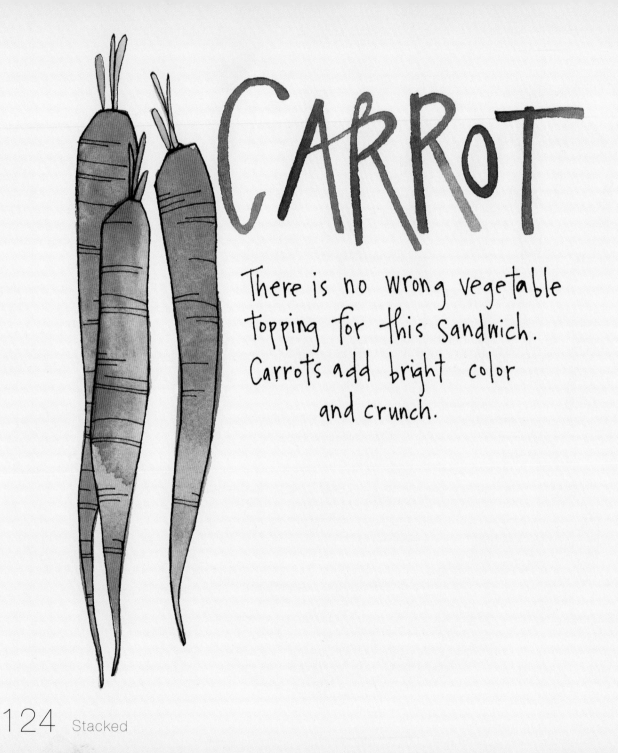

CARROT

There is no wrong vegetable topping for this sandwich. Carrots add bright color and crunch.

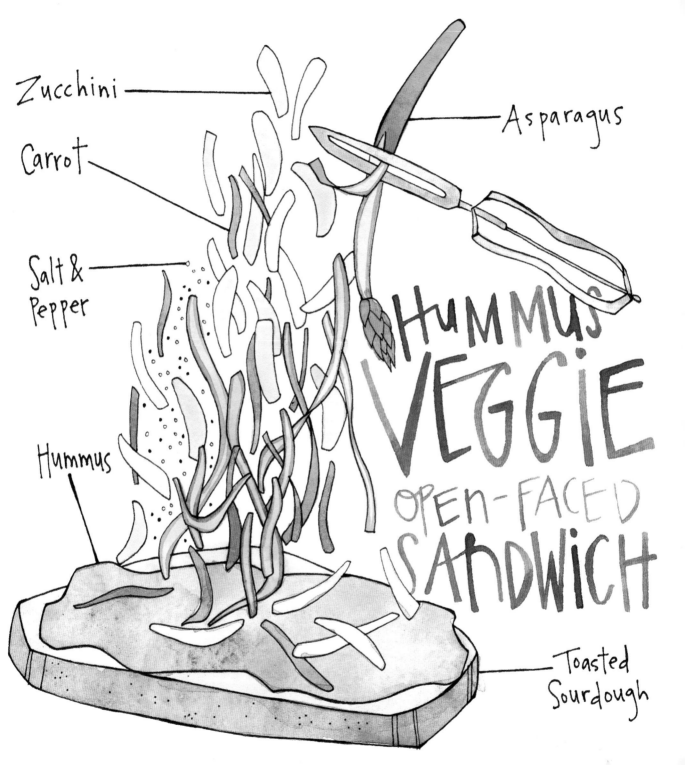

Zucchini

Carrot

Salt & Pepper

Hummus

Asparagus

HUMMUS VEGGIE OPEN-FACED SANDWICH

Toasted Sourdough

Dried figs are delicious plain.

Or dipped in chocolate.

Or stuffed with cheese.

FiG

Cut off the top of a dried fig.

Gently push back the sides.

Stuff with softened Goat Cheese & sprinkle Cinnamon on top.

or

Drizzle with melted Chocolate.

STUFFED FIG

DATE

Dates, a tiny
fruit packed with
nutrients, make a
perfect little pocket
for your favorite cheese.
They are also a good
substitute for raisins.

Stuffed Dates

Slice through one side and remove the pit.

Stuff with Blue Cheese & a chocolate chip.

Broil until cheese and chocolate just begin to melt into the date.

BROIL

Celery

Sometimes the fixins' are the best part.
Include everything but the chicken wings in
this wrap.

Shredded Lettuce

Chopped Cucumber

Shredded Carrot

Chopped Celery

Cooked Rice

Ranch dressing

Buffalo Wing Sauce

Flour Tortilla

CELERY Buffalo Ranch WRAP

Roll it up like a burrito.

Swiss Chard

There's no need for bread when Swiss chard is in season. It's sturdier than a lettuce leaf but just as versatile.

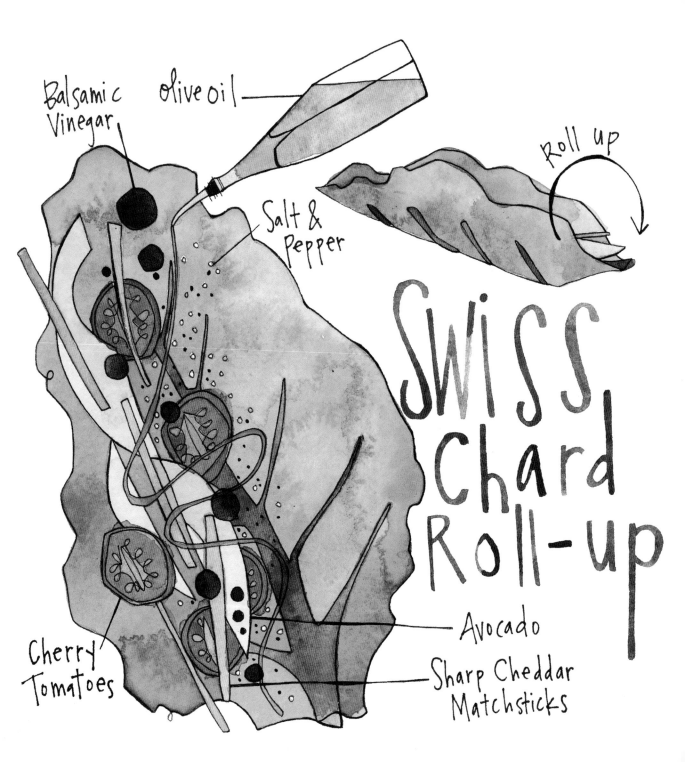

Balsamic Vinegar

olive oil

Salt & Pepper

Roll up

Cherry Tomatoes

Avocado

Sharp Cheddar Matchsticks

SWISS Chard Roll-up

GOAT CHEESE

Tangy goat cheese makes the perfect melted base to envelop sweet caramelized onions & meaty mushrooms.

Sautéed Mushrooms (page 77)

Caramelized onions (page 155)

Room temperature Goat Cheese

Flour tortilla

FOLD

GOAT CHEESE
& caramelized
onion
Quesadilla

Cook until the tortilla begins to brown and the cheese gets melty. Flip.

BiBB Lettuce

Bibb lettuce makes a great pouch for this take on Greek Salad.

Boston lettuce is another wrap alternative.

GREEK
LETTUCE
ROLL-
UP

olive oil

Cooked
Angel hair
pasta

Grape tomatoes

Salt & Pepper

Feta cheese

Red onion

cucumber

Bibb lettuce

Pull sides
together &
Enjoy.

Celery

Celery is the perfect vessel for nut butter and dried fruit. From childhood until, well, always.

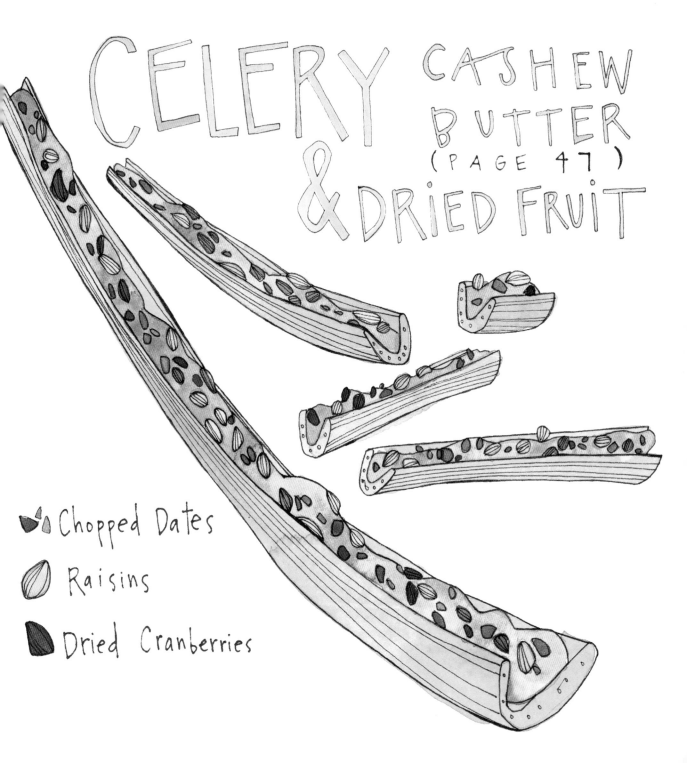

CELERY
CASHEW BUTTER (PAGE 47) & DRIED FRUIT

Chopped Dates

Raisins

Dried Cranberries

Blueberry

Dress up your pancakes with the sweetness of blueberries & corn.

Blueberry & Corn Pancakes

From last night's corn on the cob

a heaping handful

Mix up a batch of your favorite pancake batter.

Enjoy plain or with syrup & butter.

Strawberry

Pick your own strawberries; enjoy some in the field and then slice a few over ricotta.

Strawberries
with Ricotta
& Balsamic Drizzle

Plantain

Be adventurous at the grocery store. Shopping for bananas? Take a look at the plantains, usually nearby, for something new. In this recipe, make sure to get a little bit of everything on each forkful.

Cook each side until golden brown in vegetable oil.

FLIP

Place on a paper towel to soak up extra oil.

Slice a ripe plantain (the peel should be starting to turn black).

FRIED PLANTAINS WITH AVOCADO FETA MASH

Dollop of plain yogurt

Avocado mashed with feta cheese

Salt

MANGO

Not mango season?
Thaw some frozen mango chunks
before tossing everything together.

Soy Ginger Dressing (page 37)

Sliced Avocado

Cucumbers, seeded & cut into matchsticks

A batch of rice, cooked

Peeled & diced

Mango Rice Salad

Pecan

Pecans make this easy dessert look & taste F A N C Y.

Melt the chocolates in the microwave in bursts of 20 to 30 seconds, stirring until melted.

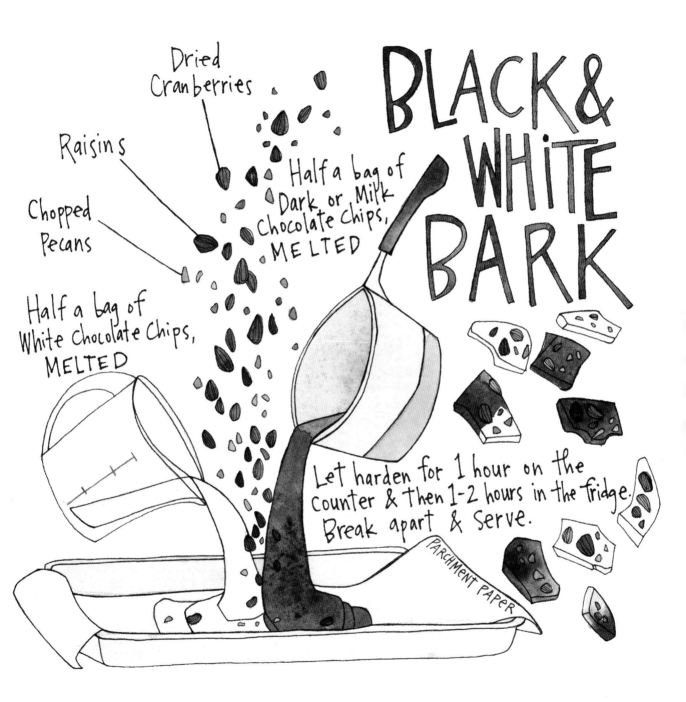

Dried Cranberries

Raisins

Chopped Pecans

Half a bag of White Chocolate Chips, MELTED

Half a bag of Dark or Milk Chocolate Chips, MELTED

BLACK & WHITE BARK

Let harden for 1 hour on the counter & then 1-2 hours in the fridge. Break apart & serve.

PARCHMENT PAPER

onion

Caramelized onions
are the ultimate topper:
baked potatoes, pizzas,
Sandwiches, salads, steaks,
just about everything.

Turn onion slices to coat in melted Butter.

Cook low & slow until the onions are gooey & caramel colored.

CaraMelized Onions

GRAPE

Add both green & red grapes to this salad for extra color.

Chopped Kale Salad with Grapes —halved

Quick Vinaigrette: olive oil & Balsamic Vinegar

Toasted pine nuts

Celery

This soup is hearty & easy, and it tastes even better the next day. Add shredded chicken to make a filling meal.

Onion

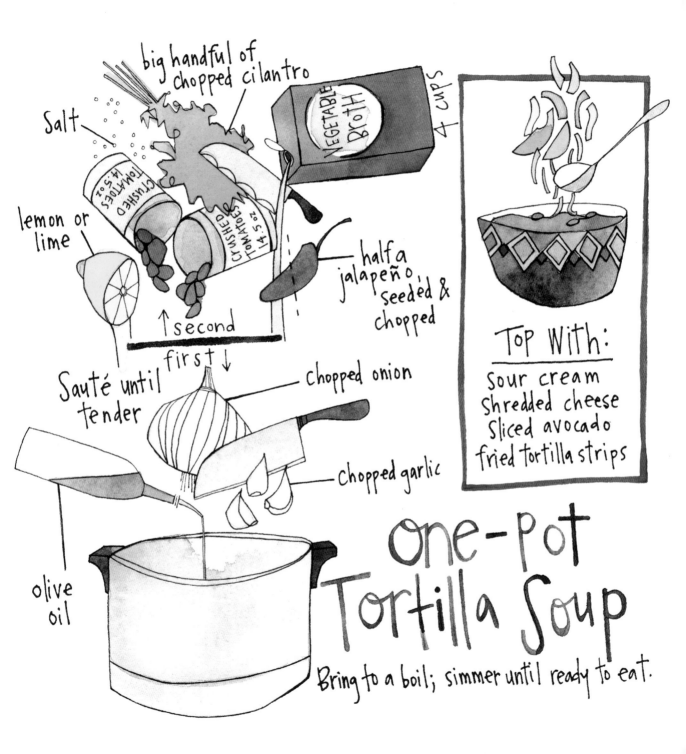

big handful of chopped cilantro

Salt

VEGETABLE BROTH

4 CUPS

CRUSHED TOMATOES 14.5 oz

lemon or lime

half a jalapeño, seeded & chopped

↑ second

first ↓

Sauté until tender

chopped onion

chopped garlic

olive oil

TOP WITH:
Sour cream
Shredded cheese
Sliced avocado
fried tortilla strips

one-pot
Tortilla Soup

Bring to a boil; simmer until ready to eat.

Cilantro

A general rule of thumb for fresh cilantro: more, please.

Roughly chop & mix with lots of Cilantro.

Grill pineapple spears until they are tender & have grill marks.

Salt

use it:
as salsa,
as fish taco topping,
OR
in a warm tortilla with fresh mozzarella

Pineapple Cilantro Salsa

Red Leicester

Kids will love this mild orange cheese as much as the adults do. It's good for melting, too.

Red Leicester cheese plate

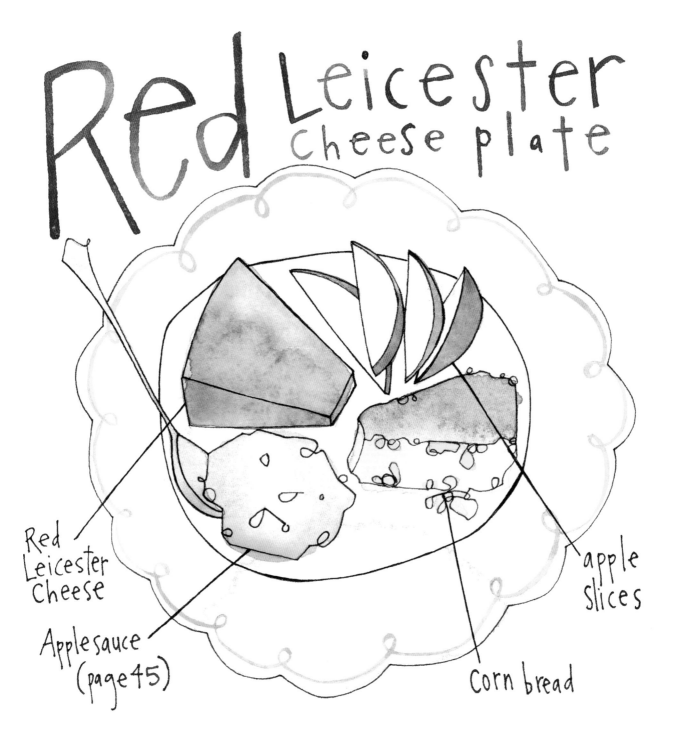

Red Leicester Cheese

Applesauce (page 45)

Corn bread

apple Slices

Blue Cheese

Pungent blue cheese is the best
supporting actor in so many dishes:
salads, dressings, on top of steaks.
Put its strong flavor in the spotlight
on a cheese plate.

Blue Cheese Plate

Crackers

Cashews

Blue Cheese

Dried Cherries

Robiola

Trying out a new cheese is the best excuse to wander through your local cheese shop. Ask questions and most definitely try samples.

ROBIOLA PLATE

Pecorino

Salty Pecorino Romano and freshly ground black pepper strike a simple balance in this homemade pasta dish. For a salty-sweet dish, try Pecorino with some juicy pear.

Cacio e Pepe

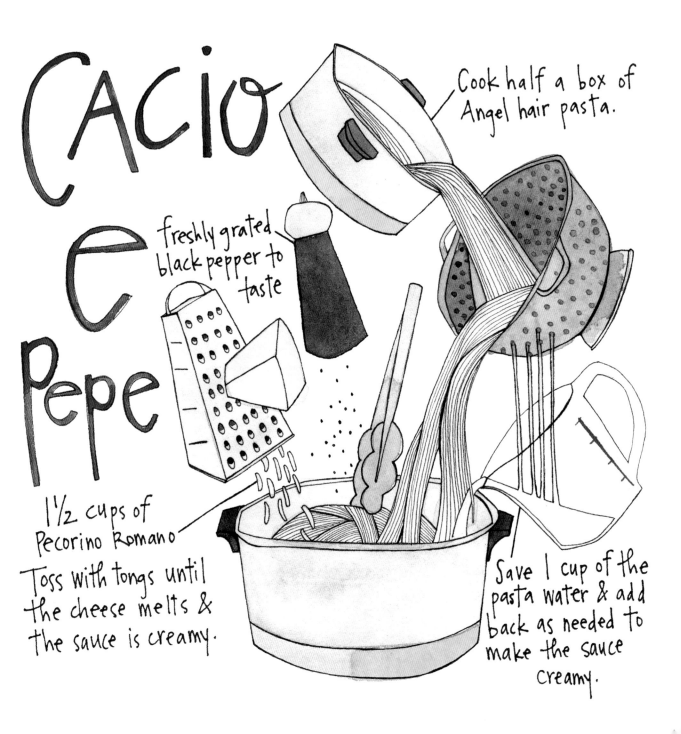

Cook half a box of Angel hair pasta.

freshly grated black pepper to taste

1½ cups of Pecorino Romano

Toss with tongs until the cheese melts & the sauce is creamy.

Save 1 cup of the pasta water & add back as needed to make the sauce creamy.

In the winter heat Halloumi on your stovetop, in the summer on your grill.

Halloumi

Grilled Halloumi

FLIP

Toasted Pepitas
(page 81)

Raisins

On medium heat,
grill Halloumi cheese
until browned on
both sides, just
a few minutes.

Fontina

Your own personal skillet of warm, gooey cheese is the best comfort food. Fontina, Gruyère, Comté, and Emmentaler all melt nicely.

Squeeze of Lemon

Second

First

handful each of Fontina & Comté cheese

Stir until melted.

FONDUE

olive oil

Sauté until tender.

shallot, chopped

garlic, chopped

Take off of the heat & use as a dip for torn up crusty bread & apple slices.

6-inch mini skillet

Ricotta

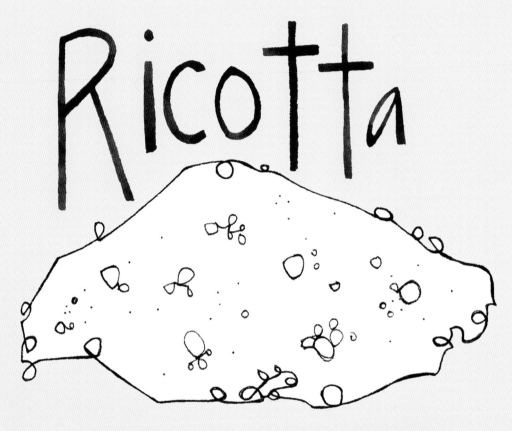

A dollop of ricotta is a good dessert
with fruit, a nice side for meatballs,
and the perfect topping for homemade crostini.

Honey
Ricotta
crostini

Coarse Kosher
Salt

(Page 93)

OTHER COMBOS
TO TRY:

Blue Cheese &
Caramelized Onion
(page 155)

Pea Purée & Ricotta
(page 51)

Feta & Honey

Mozzarella

Fresh mozzarella just tastes so good melty —— on chicken, on eggplant, on bread, on pizza. Sneak a bite while slicing it up.

Lightly butter

French or Sourdough bread

Mozzarella cheese

Ricotta cheese

OPTIONAL:
Smear some Pesto (page 35) between the cheeses.

Ricotta Mozzarella Melt

Toast on medium heat until both sides are golden brown & the cheese is melty.

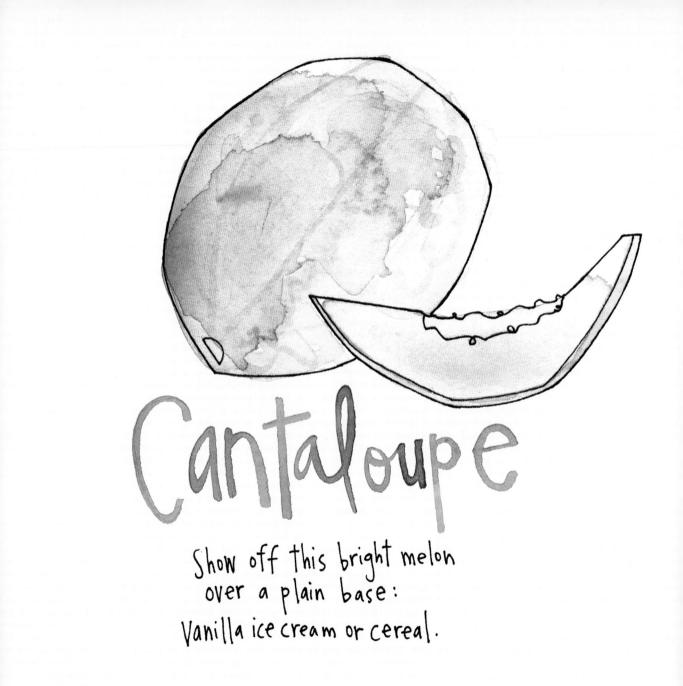

Cantaloupe

Show off this bright melon
over a plain base:
Vanilla ice cream or cereal.

Cantaloupe Blueberries & Vanilla Bean ICE Cream

Apple

Applesauce tastes just as good for dessert as it does with dinner.

Cinnamon

Warm Applesauce
(page 45)

Vanilla Bean
ice cream

Apple Pie
ice cream

Pineapple

Use your grill pan for sticky, juicy, tender seared pineapple year-round.

Grill pineapple until it is tender & has nice grill marks.

Caramel

Vanilla Bean Ice cream

Roughly chop.

Grilled Pineapple with ice cream & Caramel

Raspberry

Make this parfait in a clear jar. Enjoy the pretty colors. Fruit purée, yogurt, granola, repeat.

Raspberry Spinach Parfait

Purée

Granola
(page 87)

plain or
vanilla
yogurt

Creative Uses for Condiments, Sauces, and More

Kale Pesto (page 35) Spread on sandwiches, crostini, and pizza
Use as a sauce for eggs or fish
Toss with hot pasta

Soy Ginger Dressing (page 37) Dress stir-fried veggies
Marinate short ribs (add some garlic)

Cilantro Lime Dressing (page 39) Drizzle on sandwiches
Dip chips into a fresh batch

Sweet Vinaigrette (page 41) Dress green leafy salads
Pair with tomato, mozzarella, and basil,
in a salad or a sandwich

Applesauce (page 45) Mound on potato pancakes or
any kind of pork

Cashew Butter (page 47) Add protein to smoothies
Smear on apple slices
CB&J

Guacamole (page 49) Spread on a sandwich or toast
Dollop on eggs, tacos, or tostadas

Sautéed Mushrooms (page 77) Top pizzas, steak, greens, crostini,
and flatbread
Mix into eggs or noodles

Herb Butter (page 103)

Toss with hot pasta (try egg noodles!)
Smear on thick bread and toast under
  the broiler
Cook eggs or shrimp with it

Cheddar Pepper Spread (page 105)

Dress up crunchy veggies
Slather on crackers and biscuits
Spread on sandwiches and wraps

**Strawberries with Ricotta &
Balsamic Drizzle (page 147)**

Top biscuits, shortcake,
  or waffles

Caramelized Onions (page 155)

Pile on baked potatoes, crostini, pizza,
  and flatbreads
Layer into a toasted cheese sandwich
Add to broth for soup

Pineapple Cilantro Salsa (page 161)

Serve with chips
Spoon onto fish tacos
Roll with fresh mozzarella in a warm tortilla

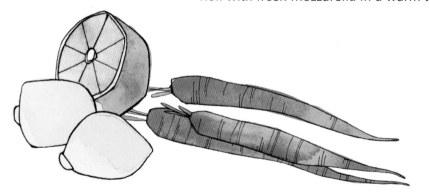

Make It a Fuller Meal

Most of the small-plate recipes in this book are vegetarian, but if you're craving a little meat (or chicken or fish) to make it a fuller meal, try one of these combos.

- Burrito Scramble (page 21) + slow cooker chicken in taco seasoning

- Green Beans & Egg (page 23) + diced ham

- Watermelon Herb Salad (page 65) + grilled skewered shrimp

- Apple Manchego Salad (page 67) + broiled crab cakes

- Spinach Salad (page 69) + steak

- Asparagus Apple Salad (page 73) + chorizo

- Asparagus Avocado Salad (page 75) + poached salmon

- Gilded Baked Potato (page 85) + grilled fish + Tomato Slices (page 111)

- Garlic Bread (page 91) + meatballs + greens + Sweet Vinaigrette (page 41)

- Egg in a Sweet Hole (page 115) + bacon

- Tostada with Beans & Feta (page 119) + shredded beef or chicken

- Celery Buffalo Ranch Wrap (page 133) + rotisserie chicken

- Swiss Chard Roll-Up (page 135) + sliced grilled chicken

- Greek Lettuce Roll-Up (page 139) + lemon garlic sautéed shrimp, diced

- Fried Plantains with Avocado Feta Mash (page 149) + black bean tacos or barbecue pulled chicken

- Mango Rice Salad (page 151) + slow cooker beef short ribs marinated in Soy Ginger Dressing (page 37) and chopped fresh garlic

- Chopped Kale Salad with Grapes (page 157) + burgers on the grill

- One-Pot Tortilla Soup (page 159) + shredded rotisserie chicken

- Cacio e Pepe (page 171) + panko, Parmesan, and herb-crusted baked chicken

- Grilled Halloumi (page 173) + steak + greens + Sweet Vinaigrette (page 41)

- Fondue (page 175) + apple chicken sausage

Acknowledgments

Thanks are due to so many people who supported this endeavor from the very beginning, first and foremost my husband, Eric. The book was inspired by our amazing little girl, Abigail, who is my favorite kitchen helper, ever. I was pregnant with our son, Jackson, during the heart of recipe creation. Thanks for cooperating during the early days, little boy, and being my very first taste tester! My family has been taste testers and cheerleaders throughout this process, at all hours and with tight deadlines; thank you. My big sister, Liz, is my best friend and knows just when I need a nudge. I wouldn't have had the guts to do this if I didn't have you in my corner, always. Thanks also to Mom, Dad, Debbie, and Jeff.

I was truly overwhelmed by the immediate and enthusiastic response of so many recipe testers; thank you for critiquing these ideas. A special thanks to my good friend Abby, who spent a few key summer days early in this endeavor brainstorming, food shopping, and lending support. Thank you to Maggie for making important introductions, first to Katie and then to Sally Ekus, my agent, who believed in my project from the get-go and helped find it a home. Thank you Margaret, my editor, for loving this concept and giving it legs. And thank you to Katie, who was so excited and agreed to do sample illustrations for me before a book proposal was even complete. This book wouldn't have come to life without you. It has been an incredible treat to work with you.

– Lauren K. Stein

Thank you to my family and friends for testing recipes using the roughest of sketches: Rick and Roxanne Eberts, Jan Wiseman, Dolores Black, Joanne Gillett, Chelsea Bashore, and Ellen Rosengard. You are all gems and I appreciate you! Thanks to Jeff Stiefel for putting together this beautiful book and dealing with me being so green-behind-the-ears and asking 12 billion questions. And thank you to Lauren for approaching me with this project. You are the most amazing collaborator and long-distance friend. Working on this cookbook with you has been such a rewarding experience, and I feel like the luckiest girl in the world. We make a pretty great team, right?!

– Katie Eberts

Index

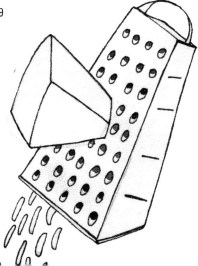

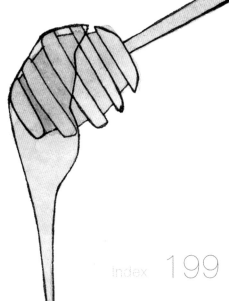

Other Storey Books You Will Enjoy

The Apple Cookbook
by Olwen Woodier

Apple pie is just the beginning. Discover the versatility of this iconic fruit with 125 delicious recipes for any meal, including apple frittata, pork chops with apple cream sauce, apple pizza, apple butter, and many more.

240 pages. Paper. ISBN 978-1-61212-518-3.

Fermented Vegetables
by Kirsten K. Shockey & Christopher Shockey

Get to work making your own kimchi, pickles, sauerkraut, and more, with this colorful and delicious guide. With beautiful photography, learn methods to ferment 64 vegetables and herbs, along with dozens of creative recipes.

376 pages. Paper. ISBN 978-1-61212-425-4.

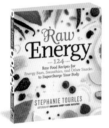

Raw Energy
by Stephanie Tourles

Supercharge your body with more than 100 recipes for delicious raw snacks: unprocessed, uncooked, simple, and pure. Use raw fruits, vegetables, nuts, seeds, and oils to make smoothies, trail mixes, energy bars, candies, and much more.

272 pages. Paper. ISBN 978-1-60342-467-7.

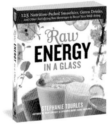

Raw Energy in a Glass
by Stephanie Tourles

Best-selling author Stephanie Tourles offers more than 120 super-nutritious, super-delicious recipes for smoothies, vegan shakes, power shots, mocktails, and more, all designed to boost your health and energy using just a standard blender.

288 pages. Paper. 978-1-61212-248-9.